CW00421420

FRANCIS FRITH'S

SUFFOLK

LIVING MEMORIES

CLIVE PAINE was born and educated in Bury St Edmunds, and apart from years at university has worked there all his life. He is a teacher, lecturer, author and broadcaster on all aspects of local history. He has taught history and local history for 30 years, 21 of which were as County Advisory Teacher for Archives and Local History in Suffolk. He has been a part-time lecturer in Local History for the Cambridge University Institute of Continuing Education for over 20 years. His publications include 'Hartest: A Village History'; 'The Culford Estate'; 'The History of Eye'; 'The Spoil of Melford Church' (with David Dymond); 'Francis Frith's Bury St Edmunds'; 'The Suffolk Bedside Book'; 'Francis Frith's Suffolk' and 'Suffolk, A Second Selection'; and 'Suffolk Villages'. He frequently broadcasts on local and national radio, and appeared with Prince Edward on his 'Crown and Country' series for ITV; he has also been profiled in Reader's Digest. He is a Council member of the Suffolk Institute of Archaeology and History, the Executive of the Suffolk Local History Council and past Chairman of the Education Committee of the British Association for Local History. He is also a Lay Reader at St Mary's in Bury.

FRANCIS FRITH'S
PHOTOGRAPHIC MEMORIES

S U F F O L K
LIVING MEMORIES

CLIVE PAINE

First published in the United Kingdom in 2004 by
Frith Book Company Ltd

Hardback Edition 2004
ISBN 1-85937-510-3

British Library Cataloguing in Publication Data

FRANCIS FRITH'S Suffolk - Living Memories
Clive Paine

Frith Book Company Ltd
Frith's Barn, Teffont,
Salisbury, Wiltshire SP3 5QP
Tel: +44 (0) 1722 716 376
Email: info@francisfrith.co.uk
www.francisfrith.co.uk

Printed and bound in Great Britain

Front Cover: **BECCLES,** *The River c1960* B45066t
Frontispiece: **LOWESTOFT,** *Children's Corner c1945* L105070

*The colour-tinting is for illustrative purposes only, and is not intended to be
historically accurate*

AS WITH ANY HISTORICAL DATABASE THE FRITH ARCHIVE IS CONSTANTLY
BEING CORRECTED AND IMPROVED, AND THE PUBLISHERS WOULD
WELCOME INFORMATION ON OMISSIONS OR INACCURACIES

CONTENTS

Acknowledgements

In preparing the captions I have visited every location to compare the archive photographs with the present day. I am grateful to so many friendly and generous people who shared their memories with me. I especially want to thank the following for their essential contributions to this book:

Peter Arbon, Rosemary Bailey, Sue Barnsley, June Brereton, Susan Brocks, John Burrage, Brian Chatters, Sue Cowling, Barbara and Ron Downey, Carole Elvin, Jim Fenning, Mary and Hedley Goddard, Bill Goodall, Anne and Mervyn Goodwin, Howard Gosnall, Ray Green, Tony Green, Joyce Hazelwood, Bill Heffer, Sheila and Ted Hills, Keith Jonceline, Ray Leek, Daphne Lloyd, Bob Malster, Ann Pryke, Carole Read, Carole and Chris Richardson, Julia Reisz, Keith Robinson, Alison Rowley, Rose Spalding, Robert Webster and Steve Williams.

Many thanks also go to Jane Cummins who, as usual, worked miracles from my handwriting to set the text, which was no mean feat.

I dedicate this book of Suffolk Memories to Christine Grayson Toms of Lavenham, who became my wife on Easter Saturday 2004.

FRANCIS FRITH
VICTORIAN PIONEER

FRANCIS FRITH, founder of the world-famous photographic archive, was a complex and multi-talented man. A devout Quaker and a highly successful Victorian businessman, he was philosophical by nature and pioneering in outlook.

By 1855 he had already established a wholesale grocery business in Liverpool, and sold it for the astonishing sum of £200,000, which is the equivalent today of over £15,000,000. Now a very rich man, he was able to indulge his passion for travel. As a child he had pored over travel books written by early explorers, and his fancy and imagination had been stirred by family holidays to the sublime mountain regions of Wales and Scotland. 'What lands of spirit-stirring and enriching scenes and places!' he had written. He was to return to these scenes of grandeur in later years to 'recapture the thousands of vivid and tender memories', but with a different purpose. Now in his thirties, and captivated by the new science of photography, Frith set out on a series of pioneering journeys up the Nile and to the Near East that occupied him from 1856 unti 1860.

INTRIGUE AND EXPLORATION

These far-flung journeys were packed with intrigue and adventure. In his life story, written when he was sixty-three, Frith tells of being held captive by bandits, and of fighting 'an awful midnight battle to the very point of surrender with a deadly pack of hungry, wild dogs'. Wearing flowing Arab costume, Frith arrived at Akaba by camel sixty years before Lawrence of Arabia, where he encountered 'desert princes and rival sheikhs, blazing with jewel-hilted swords'.

He was the first photographer to venture beyond the sixth cataract of the Nile. Africa was still the mysterious 'Dark Continent', and Stanley and Livingstone's historic meeting was a decade into the future. The conditions for picture taking confound belief. He laboured for hours in his wicker dark-room in the sweltering heat of the desert, while the volatile chemicals fizzed dangerously in their trays. Back in London he exhibited his photographs and was 'rapturously cheered' by members of the Royal Society. His reputation as a photographer was made overnight.

VENTURE OF A LIFE-TIME

Characteristically, Frith quickly spotted the opportunity to create a new business as a specialist publisher of photographs. He lived in an era of immense and sometimes violent change. For the poor in the early part of Victoria's reign work was exhausting and the hours long, and people had precious little free time to enjoy themselves. Most people had no transport other than a cart or gig at their disposal, and rarely

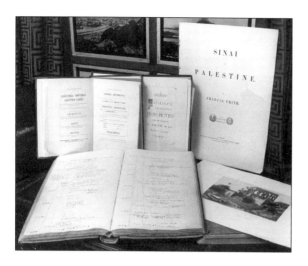

business one only has to look at the catalogue issued by Frith & Co in 1886: it runs to some 670 pages, listing not only many thousands of views of the British Isles but also many photographs of most European countries, and China, Japan, the USA and Canada - note the sample page shown on page 9 from the hand-written Frith & Co ledgers recording the pictures. By 1890 Frith had created the greatest specialist photographic publishing company in the world, with over 2,000 sales outlets - more than the combined number that Boots and WH Smith have today! The picture on the next page shows the Frith & Co display board at Ingleton in the Yorkshire Dales (left of window). Beautifully constructed with a mahogany frame and gilt inserts, it could display up to a dozen local scenes.

travelled far beyond the boundaries of their own town or village. However, by the 1870s the railways had threaded their way across the country, and Bank Holidays and half-day Saturdays had been made obligatory by Act of Parliament. All of a sudden the working man and his family were able to enjoy days out and see a little more of the world.

With typical business acumen, Francis Frith foresaw that these new tourists would enjoy having souvenirs to commemorate their days out. In 1860 he married Mary Ann Rosling and set out on a new career: his aim was to photograph every city, town and village in Britain. For the next thirty years he travelled the country by train and by pony and trap, producing fine photographs of seaside resorts and beauty spots that were keenly bought by millions of Victorians. These prints were painstakingly pasted into family albums and pored over during the dark nights of winter, rekindling precious memories of summer excursions.

THE RISE OF FRITH & CO

Frith's studio was soon supplying retail shops all over the country. To meet the demand he gathered about him a small team of photographers, and published the work of independent artist-photographers of the calibre of Roger Fenton and Francis Bedford. In order to gain some understanding of the scale of Frith's

POSTCARD BONANZA

The ever-popular holiday postcard we know today took many years to develop. In 1870 the Post Office issued the first plain cards, with a pre-printed stamp on one face. In 1894 they allowed other publishers' cards to be sent through the mail with an attached adhesive halfpenny stamp. Demand grew rapidly, and in 1895 a new size of postcard was permitted called the court card, but there was little room for illustration. In 1899, a year after Frith's death, a new card measuring 5.5 x 3.5 inches became the standard format, but it was not until 1902 that the divided back came into being, so that the address and message could be on one face and a full-size illustration on the other. Frith & Co were in the vanguard of postcard development: Frith's sons Eustace and Cyril continued their father's monumental task, expanding the number of views offered to the public and recording more and more places in Britain, as the coasts and countryside were opened up to mass travel.

Francis Frith had died in 1898 at his villa in Cannes, his great project still growing. The archive he created continued in business for another seventy years. By 1970 it contained over a third of a million pictures showing 7,000 British towns and villages.

FRANCIS FRITH'S LEGACY

Frith's legacy to us today is of immense significance and value, for the magnificent archive of evocative photographs he created provides a unique record of change in the cities, towns and villages throughout Britain over a century and more. Frith and his fellow studio photographers revisited locations many times down the years to update their views, compiling for us an enthralling and colourful pageant of British life and character.

We are fortunate that Frith was dedicated to recording the minutiae of everyday life. For it is this sheer wealth of visual data, the painstaking chronicle of changes in dress, transport, street layouts, buildings, housing, engineering and landscape that captivates us so much today. His remarkable images offer us a powerful link with the past and with the lives of our ancestors.

THE VALUE OF THE ARCHIVE TODAY

Computers have now made it possible for Frith's many thousands of images to be accessed almost instantly. Frith's images are increasingly used as visual resources, by social historians, by researchers into genealogy and ancestry, by architects and town planners, and by teachers involved in local history projects.

In addition, the archive offers every one of us an opportunity to examine the places where we and our families have lived and worked down the years. Highly successful in Frith's own era, the archive is now, a century and more on, entering a new phase of popularity. Historians consider the Francis Frith Collection to be of prime national importance. It is the only archive of its kind remaining in private ownership. Francis Frith's archive is now housed in an historic timber barn in the beautiful village of Teffont in Wiltshire. Its founder would not recognize the archive office as it is today. In place of the many thousands of dusty boxes containing glass plate negatives and an all-pervading odour of photographic chemicals, there are now ranks of computer screens. He would be amazed to watch his images travelling round the world at unimaginable speeds through internet lines.

The archive's future is both bright and exciting. Francis Frith, with his unshakeable belief in making photographs available to the greatest number of people, would undoubtedly approve of what is being done today with his lifetime's work. His photographs depicting our shared past are now bringing pleasure and enlightenment to millions around the world a century and more after his death.

SUFFOLK
AN INTRODUCTION

Suffolk is bounded by the River Stour on the south and the River Waveney to the north. In this collection the communities are represented by Sudbury and East Bergholt in the south and Beccles and Bungay to the north. To the west are Breckland and the chalk lands of Cambridgeshire, here represented by Eriswell, Lakenheath, Mildenhall, Exning and Newmarket. To the east are the coastal towns of Lowestoft, Southwold, Leiston, Aldeburgh and Felixstowe, and the villages of Kessingland,

Covehithe, Sizewell, Thorpeness and Orford. Of these villages, Covehithe and Orford were once thriving ports which silted up in the 15th century; Thorpeness was created as a seaside resort in the early 20th century; and Sizewell is known only for the power station and the teashop.

There are also river estuaries: Southwold, Walberswick and Blythburgh lie on the Blyth, which can only be crossed by a ferry, or the bridge, at Blythburgh; Aldeburgh lies on the Ald;

ALDEBURGH, *The Children's Boating Pool and the Moot Hall c1955* A28062

Waldringfield, Woodbridge and Melton on the Deben; and Trimley, Shotley, Freston and Ipswich on the Orwell.

From the 1950s the north-eastern part of the coast, from Dunwich to Corton, became an area of holiday camps, caravan parks and camping sites. At Corton, Rogerson Hall was always thought of as the most luxurious of all the holiday camps. At Kessingland, the caravan park is near the Sailors Home pub. Further south, Aldeburgh Church Farm Park is between the coast and the River Ald. The fishing industry is recorded at Lowestoft and Aldeburgh; sailing at Beccles, Waldringfield, Thorpeness, Orford and Felixstowe; and ship building and repair at Southwold and Woodbridge. The Royal Naval Training Establishment HMS Ganges was based at Shotley from 1905 until 1976.

Along the coast, the photographs record the various towns and villages which have become seaside retreats and resorts. Southwold, Aldeburgh and Lowestoft had long been famed for the curative powers of sea bathing. Lowestoft was developed by Sir Samuel Morton Peto in the 1840s and 1850s, and Felixstowe by Colonel George Tomline in the 1870s. They both built houses for residents and visitors; built a railway to bring in trade and tourists; and created docks and harbours to bring trade and employment. Lowestoft was described in 1886 as 'the very pink of propriety'. Felixstowe, following the visit of the German Empress in 1891, was known as 'the Queen of the East Coast Resorts'.

The areas of Southwold, Walberswick and Aldeburgh that we see in the photographs in this book have changed very little, and remain genteel, cultured and almost timeless. Walberswick, in the late Victorian and Edwardian period, was the home of a colony of artists, including Philip Street and Charles Rennie Mackintosh. Aldeburgh is now the home of the annual Festival started in 1948 by Benjamin Britten. Dunwich is famous for fish and chips and disappearing into the sea. Thorpeness is another purpose-built seaside village in the tiny hamlet of Thorpe in Aldringham. It was built between 1910 and 1928 as a 'garden village and model holiday hamlet by the sea'. This timber-framed black and white Tudor fantasy was the creation of Glencain Stuart Ogilvie of Sizewell Hall.

The medieval and Tudor timber-framed jettied houses in Suffolk towns and villages are as much part of the landscape as the trees from which they were constructed. In the 18th century, many houses were re-fronted in plaster or brick to give them a more modern appearance. From the 1960s onwards, the trend developed (now mainly halted) of exposing the whole timber framing, revealing far more than was intended by the original builders. The photographs of towns and village streets all include timber-framed and re-fronted timber buildings, but none is surpassed by Debenham, Lavenham, Brent Eleigh, Kersey and Hadleigh. The style was imitated in the concrete and breeze-block houses at Thorpeness.

Brick has been used since the 15th century, and very widely in the 18th and 19th centuries. There are examples of houses built or re-fronted in brick in the majority of the street scenes. There are also some outstanding brick buildings, including Woodbridge Shire Hall of c1670; the Rutland Arms, designed by John Kent in 1815, at Newmarket; and the Angel at Bury. Other buildings, such as the Aldeburgh Moot Hall of c1540 and the reconstructed De Vere house in Lavenham, combine timber with brickwork.

Suffolk was a county of landed estates, many of

which remain today. Houses on these estates were of a high quality, although often of unconventional design. At Somerleyton, Sir Samuel Morton Peto built thatched mock-Tudor cottages around a village green; at Walsham le Willows, the Martineau family built timber-framed houses carved with improving sayings and Biblical texts; while at Easton, the Duke of Hamilton built cottages with Gothic pointed windows and rustic openwork porches.

The photographs include many churches and historic sites. Lavenham, often described as the most complete medieval town, has some of the most magnificent timber houses in England. The powerful abbey of Bury St Edmunds was gradually demolished after 1539, leaving only a romantic ruin today. The castle-like Abbey Gate, of the 1340s, is a wonderful example of decorated architecture. Orford Castle, built between 1165 and 1173, was the first to be built without a square keep. Just off Southwold, under the command of the Duke of York, an English and French Fleet fought off the Dutch at the Battle of Sole Bay in 1672.

The agricultural character of the county is shown by the markets still flourishing at Woodbridge, Bungay, Sudbury, Stowmarket, Bury and Mildenhall; the three latter were photographed on market day. Bungay and Mildenhall retain their covered market crosses. Mills were still a common sight, represented here by the water and steam mill at Wickham market and by post mills at Saxstead, Holton and Thorpeness, the latter used to pump water for the village water supply.

Suffolk is the home of two major artists. Thomas Gainsborough (1727-88) was born at Sudbury. He lived in Friars Street from 1748 to 1752, where two of his daughters were born - they

WALBERSWICK, *The Green c1965* W7082

were painted in 'The Artist's Daughters Chasing a Butterfly' (1756). John Constable (1776-1837) was born at East Bergholt. The villages along the Stour valley between Nayland and Flatford are known as Constable Country, where his churches, rivers, landscapes, clouds and vast sky all remain to be seen today.

In many rural areas in the 1950s, water still came from wells; there was neither sewerage nor electricity - the privy and oil lamps were used instead. However, most towns had piped water, sewerage and electricity. In 1951, 28% of Suffolk homes were without piped water, 34% without WCs and 53% without fixed baths. By 1971, all had piped water; only 4% were without WCs, and 11% without baths.

In 1955 the vast majority of parishes still had a resident clergyman at the rectory or vicarage. The village school, usually dating from the Victorian period, was still open. The village shops, one of which was the post office, served the needs of the locals without the threat of competition of supermarkets. The village pubs, in the days before pub food, carpets and muzak, provided real ale, traditional entertainment and a sense of community. The photographs show shops, post offices, Co-operative stores, butchers, bakers, blacksmiths, drapers, grocers, pubs, hotels and a wider variety of shops in the towns.

The greatest changes in Suffolk were to come after 1955. These were mainly losses, including the loss of railway links in the Beeching cuts after 1963; of shops in towns and villages, due to the supermarkets; of village schools, due to the declining child population, such as the ones in Blaxhall and Butley; of village crafts, as their need and use abated; and of pubs, due to the closure and amalgamation of breweries – Eye, for exam-

ple, had 11 pubs in 1940 and now has only one.

From the 1960s onwards, the population rose so as to make Suffolk one of the fastest-growing areas of the British Isles. Between 1961 and 1986 the population increased by 34%, of which 90% was due to inward migration. This was stimulated by national and local planning policy, which encouraged London overspill relocation to rural areas, furthered the development of Ipswich and Felixstowe, and improved communications from the Midlands to Felixstowe Docks.

The photographs of Brandon show buildings which were demolished in order to widen roads. At Haverhill few of the buildings shown now remain, owing to the redevelopment of the High Street and Queen Street. One photograph shows the contrast between the new concrete, functional buildings of Queen's Square and what remains of Queen Street.

Massive changes were also taking place in agriculture. Between 1950 and 1980 the acreage of farms increased dramatically, reducing by half the number of farms from 8,067 to 3,922. Not only holdings but fields became larger, as the era of prairie farming, with the grubbing up of hedges, began. The number of combine harvesters rose from 42 in 1942 to 2,970 in 1968. These changes had a dramatic effect on the number of people employed in agriculture - in 1981 this was a mere 3.7% of the working population.

The photographs in this collection of Suffolk memories cover the period from about 1955 to 1965. As we have seen, this was almost the end of an era in urban and rural life. These photographs provide a record of Suffolk which enables us to see the changes in our own locality over the past 40 to 50 years.

THE SUFFOLK COAST

BUCKLESHAM, *The Shannon Inn c1955* B616007a

This building contained the village post office and the public house. The unusual name comes from the ship of Captain Philip Broke of Nacton, whose estate extended into Bucklesham. On 1 June 1813, during the war with America, Broke captured the 'Chesapeake' after a battle of only 11 minutes.

▼ **TRIMLEY,** *The Three Mariners Inn c1955* T80003

The railings of St Mary's churchyard are on the right. In the distance the post office and house remain, but the next house has been demolished. The Cobbold Ale sign, over the bay window of the 18th-century pub, has been painted over, and a new sign placed over the left-hand door. Off to the left is the Welcome Hall of 1902.

▶ **FELIXSTOWE**
The Bay Looking East c1955 F16026

The bowling green is surrounded by beach huts and set amidst suburbia in St Edmund's Road, with Cordy's Regal restaurant, now The Alex, to the right. The new pier was built in 1905 for Belle Steamers to bring holidaymakers from Ipswich, Clacton and Walton. On the horizon is St John's Church, built in 1895, with a spire added in 1913-14.

◀ **FELIXSTOWE**
The Parade 1955
F16063

The late Victorian and Edwardian buildings are part of the expansion of Felixstowe as a seaside resort. This was given impetus by the visit of the Empress of Germany and the discovery of spa water in 1891. Wakelin's (left, in Sutton House) declared itself to be 'the cycle, sport and baby carriage store of the county'.

▶ **FELIXSTOWE**
The Sands c1955
F16049

This shows the area from Convalescent Hill to Cobbold's Point, which is named after the Ipswich family who built a house there in 1829. Facing Undercliff Road are (from left to right) the 1930s Trent's Café; the Town Hall of 1892; the Empire Café; Bent Hill; and the Felix Hotel of 1903, with the Spa Pavilion of 1909 below.

▶ **ALDERTON**
The Street
c1955 A342002

The white-painted brick Tolly-owned, Crown Inn (right) closed in the 1960s. The 17th-century Cobbold Swan Inn opposite was saved from closure following a Save Our Swan campaign in 1995-1997. Beyond is the old post office, which still retains the original sign on the wall.

◀ **ALDERTON**
The Street c1955
A342007

This row contained a general and sweet shop (note the Oxo advertisement in the window), with another general store and a teashop at the far end. The brick building between is still called London House, a sure clue to a former shop – there is another London House at Ixworth. Now all the shops have closed except for the one directly ahead.

▲ **WALDRINGFIELD,** *The Yacht Club c1955* W438019

Waldringfield Sailing Club was founded in 1921. The club house, with its central lookout station, was built in 1935. To the left of it, within the fence, is the warning siren. The crowds are probably watching the annual regatta. The two ladies in the distance have just come down from the May Bush Inn.

◄ **MARTLESHAM**
The Street c1955 M267001

The lady on the left is leaving the single-storey extension containing the post office and posting box. Post Office Lane runs off to the left, level with the bus stop. The rear wing of the furthest house has now been raised to two storeys. On the opposite corner is the garage.

▼ MARTLESHAM

The Hill c1955 M267007

The Red Lion (right) dates from c1580, and has an oriel window similar to those on the Ancient House in Ipswich. The pub figurehead gave rise to the phrase 'As red as a Martlesham lion'. Opposite are the early 18th-century Red Lion Cottages, which have the same barge boards as the pub. The whole frontage has now been railed off from the road.

▶ WOODBRIDGE

The River Deben c1965
W128086

This view was taken from the railway footbridge, looking towards the famous tide mill on the left. The boat yard is a hive of activity, with cranes, men and a vessel drawn up for repair. Amongst the boats in the foreground are two Dutch fishing vessels.

WOODBRIDGE
The Crown Corner c1955 W128021

The Crown Inn (left), established in 1652, stands on the corner of the Thoroughfare, with the Cross on the opposite side. The tall building on the left has an Arts and Crafts-style gable and windows. Beyond Bakers Lane (centre left), what used to be the tearooms have become an antiques shop. Half way up on the right is the 18th-century red brick Arnot House.

▶ WOODBRIDGE
The Thoroughfare c1965
W128074

Woolworth's (right) have occupied this shop since the 1950s. The shop used to be occupied by Rowland's, an ironmonger's, cabinetmaker's and furniture warehouse. This unusual building is of metal construction very much like railway station architecture, with showroom windows above. On the left the International Stores have closed; the pinnacles beyond are on Lloyds Bank, and the gable between is Alexander's, a tailor's and outfitter's.

WOODBRIDGE
Market Place c1955
W128036

The red brick Shire Hall of c1600 once had an open ground floor – it was filled in during the 19th century. The van (right) belongs to Banyard's the butcher's, whose shop was in nearby Church Street. The buildings remain much the same, but all the businesses have changed today. The front of Blake's has been replaced, with the door now to the right.

WOODBRIDGE, *The Old Pump c1965* W128055

The pump, with its stone Gothic-style pump house and metal wheel, is dated 1876. Four metal flag finials have since been added to the corners. Off to the left is the King's Head Inn. The buildings are unchanged, but the baker's and the hardware shop have both been closed.

MELTON
The Street c1965
M268024

Skoulding's shop (to the left) now has a window across the whole building. The doors and windows have been altered on the next pair of cottages, whilst the white Rosemary Cottage and the brick gable end beyond remain unchanged. The row contains a variety of former shop fronts. Part of the building on the right has now been demolished.

MELTON, *Station Road c1965* M268021

Note the sign on the left to three RAF bases (Bawdsey, Woodbridge and Bentwaters); these were used by the Americans, and have now all closed. The building on the right was part of Skoulding's provisions shop (a different shop to that in the photo above). The dark façade hides an 18th-century timber-framed house. Set back behind the railings beyond is The Rosery, a red brick house of c1750, which stands opposite the parish church.

◀**ORFORD**
The Quay c1965 O20086

Here the shingle beach is thick with pleasure sailing boats of various types and sizes. The two girls seem reluctant to help their father with the boat. The marine landing craft in the foreground belongs to the Atomic Weapons Research Establishment, which was based at Orford Ness from 1959 until 1971.

◄ **BUTLEY**
The School c1955
B618007

The inscription on the front reads 'National and Infants School 1842'. The school was extended in 1886, and could then cater for 135 pupils from Butley and Capel St Andrew. The building is now a private house: the porch has been demolished and the canteen (right), with its gable removed, has been converted into a garage.

▲ **ORFORD,** *Market Square c1965* O20074

This view, looking west, shows E J Pipe's general store smothered in advertisements (left). This is now the Butley Oysterage, and the bay window has been removed. The earlier Oysterage, next door, has become an antiques shop. The market is dominated by the castle (centre right), which was built by Henry II between 1165 and 1173. The scaffolding shows that it is under repair by the Ministry of Works.

◄ **ORFORD**
Market Square and Church c1965 O20025

A market was held here from 1154 until the 19th century. On the left is the corner of the brick-fronted manor house. The top of the church tower fell in 1829, which gave it a castle-like appearance. It was not restored until the 1960s. The absence of cars in the square might indicate a Sunday morning.

▶ **PETTISTREE**
The Church c1960 P391036

The 15th-century tower has flushwork patterns on the buttresses and parapet. The eastern buttresses are unusual in that they are extensions of the nave west wall. Below the nave roof is a row of blocked quatrefoil windows, although the aisles were never built. The chancel and vestry date from 1894.

◀ **WICKHAM MARKET**
The Mill c1960 W94041

The mill has been owned by the Rackham family for several generations; they were maltsters, water and steam millers, and animal food and coal merchants. The tower of the steam engine house has now been demolished. The water mill is 18th-century, with three pairs of wheels driven by a cast iron breast-shot wheel.

▶ **WICKHAM MARKET**
The Hill c1960
W94040

The central area, with car park and bus shelter, was redesigned in 2002. On the left is the Georgian-fronted White Hart Hotel. The former Crown Inn is at the end of the row (centre), beneath the octagonal church tower with its wooden leaded spire. To the right, the building with a hipped roof is now three shops.

◀ **EASTON**
The Village c1950
E244001

The 16th-century house with Victorian windows and a rustic timber porch (left) was where the agent to the Duke of Hamilton lived. The White Horse (centre) was built in two stages in the late 16th and early 17th centuries. The lower section has Victorian gothic dormer windows. In the distance are Pump Cottage and Lavender Cottage, both built in mock-Tudor style.

▲ **BLAXHALL,** *The Youth Hostel c1960* B614002

This was the village school, built in 1881 by John Sheppard. George Ewart Evans came to live in Blaxhall in 1948, when his wife became headmistress. He did much of his early oral history recording in the village; this formed the basis of many books, including 'Ask the Fellows who Cut the Hay' in 1956.

◀ **FRAMLINGHAM**
Bridge Street c1955 F45011

A range of houses this side of the telegraph pole has been demolished. The two ladies are at the turning to Maulden's Mill, whilst the children are outside Brackenbury's Tarpaulins. The church tower is 96 feet high, with large windows, battlements, and lions instead of corner pinnacles.

FRAMLINGHAM
Market Hill c1955 F45005

The jettied Crown Hotel (left) dates from c1550, with a Victorian mock-Tudor front. The central archway is now filled in with a wooden Gothic-style door. The Victorian Barclay's Bank beyond has delightful carved heads over the door and windows. Beyond is No 26, now William Brown, which has the best timber framing in the town. The hairdresser's shop of C Moore (straight ahead) has become a restaurant, whose frontage now includes the right-hand window. Is the military jeep (centre) waiting for the horse and tumbrel to move?

SAXSTEAD, *The Windmill c1955* S578001

This post mill ceased working in 1947, but its fabric and machinery are maintained by English Heritage. It is thought that a mill has stood here for 700 years. Situated on the edge of Saxstead Green, this is one of the best-known landmarks in Suffolk.

RENDHAM
The White Horse c1960
R326013

To the left is the now closed red brick post office, whose shop front has been replaced by three windows. Ahead is the 17th-century timber-framed White Horse and the Victorian South View Cottage. The road to the left leads to the former Independent Chapel of 1750. The parish church of St Michael is to our right.

SAXMUNDHAM, *South Approach c1955* S69005

The trees on the left are at the entrance to Hurts Hall, a mock-Elizabethan mansion of 1893. The row of buildings beyond includes Nichol's the undertaker's and Ashford's Furniture Depository. Hunter & Oliver the wine merchant's (right) was established c1940; the shop succeeded the Waller family's shop, which had been here at least since 1844. The petrol pump stands in front of Smith & Wesby's garage.

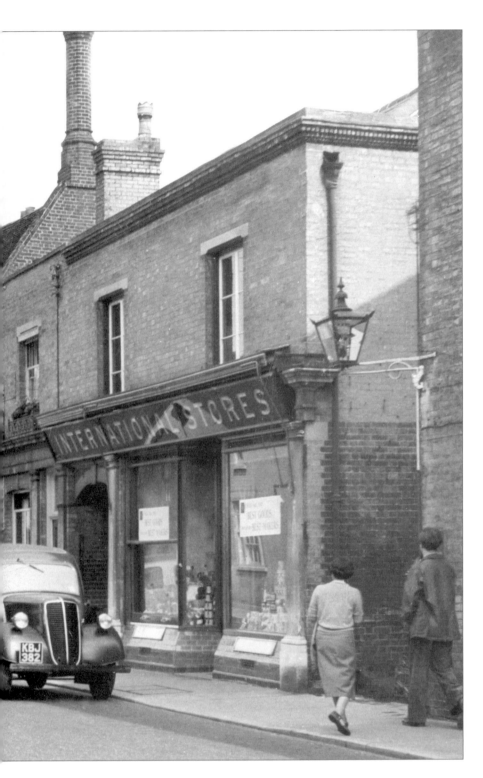

SAXMUNDHAM
High Street c1955
S69009

The International Stores (right) has had a shop here since c1900, but by 1986 it had become Gateway. The White Hart beyond, with its tall chimneys, was run by Dick Powling as a family and commercial hotel. The gabled HSBC next door began as the London and Provincial Bank in 1908. The shop with awnings was Alex Martin's, a draper's. The former King's Head in the distance was Ashford's the furnisher's from c1850 until 1982.

▼ **SAXMUNDHAM,** *High Street c1955* S69021

Ely's fish and chip shop (left) on the corner of Chantry Road has a Dutch gable. Beyond is the sign for Clarke's Tea Room, and then the Co-op, built in 1932. The buildings on the corner of Church Street were owned by Hayward & Sons, who traded from the adjacent shop (right). In the distance is Ashford House, the former King's Head Inn.

► **SAXMUNDHAM**
Market Place
c1955 S69017

At the end of the street is Gardener's, the gents' outfitter's. On the right is the Oddfellows Office, here since 1933, and Barker's, fishmongers since 1946. The fine bay window next to Proudfoot's the tobacconist's has now gone. The sign beyond Proudfoot's is for the Angel Inn, which was kept by Mrs Emsden until its closure in 1976.

◄ ALDEBURGH
High Street c1955
A28095

This view was taken from the first floor of the present Regatta Restaurant. In the distance Crabbe Street, named after the local poet the Rev George Crabbe, who inspired the work of Benjamin Britten, leads down to the beach and the lifeboat station. The East Suffolk Hotel (the white building, centre right) is now the Aldeburgh Festival Office.

► ALDEBURGH
The Children's Boating Pool and the Moot Hall c1955 A28062

Model sailing boats ply back and forth across the pool. In the background is the Moot Hall of c1540; in front is the war memorial, now surrounded by a garden. This area was originally the market place, with streets now lost to the sea running parallel on the right. The mock-timber building on the left is the Mill Inn. Beyond it are Moot House, Market Cross Place and the White Lion.

▶ **ALDEBURGH**
The Lifeboat and Crag Path c1965 A28143

Until the 1990s, this was one of the few places where the lifeboat was kept on the open beach. Further along Crag Path is the former red and white brick watchtower (centre). On the right is a later extension to the Jubilee Hall of 1889. The white bow-fronted house is Mizpah of 1877, and beyond is High House of 1879.

◄ ALDEBURGH
The Camping Ground
c1955 A28027

Church Farm Caravan Park, now Holiday Park, is situated between Thorpeness Road and the River Ald. The river is seen here on the right, with the RSPB marshland reserve beyond. The basic layout of the camp remains much the same today, with the reception building in the centre of the tree line.

▶ **THORPENESS**
The Village
c1955 T38013

This mock-Tudor building was the Dunes Guesthouse, built in 1914 as part of a model middle-class seaside resort, which was designed by Glencain Stuart Ogilvie between 1910 and 1928. The wall to the left, now higher, marks the edge of Barn Hall of 1925, the Estate Office.

◀ **THORPENESS**
The House in the Clouds and the Mill
c1955 T38010

The water supply to Thorpeness was provided by piston pumps operated by the windmill. This is a post mill, like the one at Saxstead; it dates from 1803, and it was moved here from nearby Aldringham in 1923. The water was stored in the tank, now disused, forming the top storey of the House in the Clouds.

▲ **THORPENESS,** *Festival Singing at the Meare c1955* T38005

The 65-acre Meare (the correct spelling at fantasy Thorpeness) was dug out of marshland to provide a boating lake for children. The water is less than a yard deep, and all the bays and islands are named in J M Barrie style. A boathouse was built in 1911, which here provides the foreground for this unusual setting for a concert.

◀ **LEISTON**
The Forge c1960 L33029

The house to the left has been rebuilt, and the one to the right rendered over. The former forge building is now an estate agent's. The door and central window remain, but the wide entrance door has been blocked. The forge remains inside the building, and the sign still stands in the forecourt.

LEISTON
High Street c1960
L33014

This is the lower end of the High Street, with the Long Shop complex off to the right and Victoria Road to the left. Baker Brothers (left), originally gents' outfitters and grocers, have traded here since 1876. The other shops, G W Hales, a chemist's, W Clouting's china shop, and Leiston Abbey Press in the mock-Tudor building, have all closed.

SIZEWELL, *The Nuclear Power Station c1965* S582039

Suffolk had a new landmark with the building of Sizewell A. It was later decided to build a second Sizewell B and a third Sizewell C. Sizewell B was actually constructed, but Sizewell C was cancelled. Near where we stand is a tearoom known locally as Sizewell T, which rivals Dunwich and Aldeburgh with the quality of its fish and chips.

DUNWICH
The Ship Hotel c1965
D173078

This red brick building is dated 1868 on the gable end. The 18th-century white plastered house is the former Town Hall, reminding us of the town's former borough status. The next three cottages, including the former post office, are dated 1770, but they may be older. At the end is the Museum in the former Victorian Reading Room.

WESTLETON, *The Village Green and the Pump c1965* W441027

Off to the left is the village and the pond, famous for its ducks. One of the benches records that 18 lime trees were planted in memory of the men who died in the First World War. The former forge has become Gallery Cottage, now with a raised central gable. Pond House has the former village pump outside, here being used by two children.

YOXFORD
The Jubilee Seat c1955
Y16012

This view of the 1935 Silver Jubilee seat is taken from outside the King's Head on the A12, looking down the High Street. The horse chestnut was grown from a chestnut from Verdun, collected by Mrs Lomax of Grove Park. It was planted on 11 November 1923 by Ezra Cotton and George Davy, the oldest and youngest children at the school, to commemorate the great battles of 1916.

▼ **PEASENHALL,** *The View from the Church Tower c1955* P287007

Smyth's Peasenhall works, where the famous agricultural drills were made, is off to the right. The house to the left is a former 16th-century farmhouse, now divided into three dwellings. Stuart House, the left-hand wing, was the scene in 1902 of the murder of Rose Harsant; this still unsolved crime became known as the Peasenhall Murder Case.

▶ **BRAMFIELD**
*Bramfield Street
c1960* B878002

The view is dominated by the gents' loos of the Queen's Head (left), which were demolished in 1982-83. The roof of the Old Vicarage rises behind. The garage (centre) has been without petrol pumps since 1995. The Swan Inn, beyond, closed in the 1930s and is now called Carisbrook. In the distance is a row of mock-Tudor cottages.

WALBERSWICK
The Green c1965
W7082

The taller building straight ahead was Manor House Dairy, supplying butter, cheese and eggs. To the left is the hall of the first WI to be established in East Suffolk - it started in September 1918. The WI Hall and George Roger's garage next door are now gift shops. The red brick house next to the garage was already the Pottery Shop when this photograph was taken.

▶ **WALBERSWICK**
The River c1960
W7056

This view shows Southwold harbour on the other side of the river, with sailing craft, repair shops and landing stages. The river could be crossed by a rowing boat ferry, which replaced a Victorian steam ferry, after the Second World War. A hut very similar to this one, but at Waldringfield, was offered for sale as a holiday home in 2002 for £60,000.

BLYTHBURGH
The Village c1955
B125005

On the other side of the church lie the marshes of the Blyth estuary, which is why this magnificent church is known as the Queen of the Marshes. On Sunday 4 August 1577, the church was 'visited' by a thunderstorm and a black dog - during the visitation two members of the congregation died. The 17th-century Church Farm (centre), with its brick end wall and gables, was thatched at the time of the photograph.

WENHASTON, *The Village c1955* W440002

The Compasses Inn (left) closed in 2001, and is now being converted into a conference centre. The warehouse-like double-gabled building (centre) is the former Post Office, which closed in 2000. The house with the slated hipped roof beyond is faced with tiny flints, with brick quoins and door and window surrounds. This is very similar to the 1840s school at nearby Westleton, and was probably built by the same builder.

WAVENEY

HALESWORTH, *Market Place c1955* H384009

The King's Arms, then run by R G Wood, has closed,
but the arms remain on the present carpet shop.
Beyond is the brick Lloyds Bank of 1896. The increasing
sizes and numbers of vehicles led to the town centre
being by-passed. The building behind the man on the
Corgi (centre right) has been demolished to create
Angel Link.

HALESWORTH
Bridge Street c1955
H384006

The end of the street has changed: the gabled building on the left and the adjacent one with the awning have been demolished. The shop with the clock, at this date called The Shoe People, still sells shoes. The shop front at Fairweather's next door has been extended across the entire width of the building. On the right is the British Legion Club.

HALESWORTH, *The Thoroughfare c1955* H384007

Like Bridge Street, this is now pedestrianised. Rodwell's the solicitor's, on the left, has been lowered to two storeys. On the right is the former Guildhall of St John Baptist, St Loye and St Anthony. Advertisements in the street include Perth Dye Works, Calor gas, Philips Rubbers and Ever Ready batteries.

HOLTON, *The Mill c1960* H383031

This mid 18th-century post mill has 'I Swan 1749', 'W Bedwell' and 'John Swan 1754' carved on the beams. The mill was restored in 1966-68. The tarred brick roundhouse and fantail are Victorian; the roundhouse has two storeys, one of which is below ground level. The machinery and stones were removed c1900.

▼ **SOUTHWOLD,** *Park Lane c1960* S168046

On the right is the 1894 School of Industrial Art, built in Arts and Crafts style, with an inscription by William Tooke. The school provided off-season craftwork for 50 fishermen until it closed in1914. The bay windows and porch of the adjoining house have now been removed and the building re-fronted. James Maggs (who died in 1890), the Southwold diarist, lived opposite.

▶ **SOUTHWOLD**
St James' Green and the Lighthouse c1955
S168028

The single-storey white building was the Coastguard Station, built between 1884 and 1904. Beacon Cottage, to the left, takes its name from the beacon that preceded the lighthouse of 1890. Blyth House next door has been reduced to two storeys, and now looks like an eight-bay Georgian house.

◄ **SOUTHWOLD**
The Town Hall and High Street c1960
S168087

The central lamp standard dates from 1873: the globe is supported by fishes and surmounted with the crown and arrows of St Edmund, to whom the church is dedicated. The Swan, the Town Hall next door and F C Munt, the chemist's (on the corner, left of centre) are unchanged, but the shop between is now Somerfield's. The banner across the street in the distance is for the annual art exhibition.

► **SOUTHWOLD**
High Street c1955
S168026

The seven-bay Crown Hotel (right), with columned porch, has a large and elaborate sign over the street. The painted advertisement next door has gone, but the gable beyond retains the date 1662. Beyond Barclays bank, on the left, the United Reformed Church is set back from the street. A cluster of bus signs has begun to gather on the left.

SOUTHWOLD
High Street c1955 S168044

The Post Office (right) was situated here for a few years after a fire in 1952 at the present Post Office, which was caused by petrol hoarding during the Suez Crisis. The cinema (centre left) closed in the 1960s. To the right, the Coffee House is now a domestic garage, but the house is still called Jack o'Lantern.

SOUTHWOLD
The Pier Entrance
c1955 S168032

This was built in the 1930s to replace a wooden structure, and the pier was restored in 1998. On the ground floor the horizontal windows remain, but all the others have been altered. The figure of Neptune on the first floor has gone. The handrails are covered with small plaques, with messages and dedications from the subscribers.

WRENTHAM, *Cross Roads c1965* W444013

The brick school-like building is the former Reading Room of 1888, now appropriately a bookshop. Beyond is the Gothic pinnacled Wrentham Hall of 1862. The Jubilee Clock of 1897 (just visible on the central gable), given by Sir Alfred Gooch of Benacre Hall, has been removed. Wrentham Stores (right) has closed, but Broadways, beyond, remains.

COVEHITHE, *The Church c1960* C515018

This unusual view is taken through the east window of the south aisle, with the chancel to the right. As the village gradually declined as the port silted up, so its large and impressive church was reduced in size. Only the tower survives intact, and the brick nave was built inside the ruin in 1672.

▼ **KESSINGLAND,** *The Beach c1960* K137021

While a group of children on the beach greet the photographer, others visit the sweet shop (left), whilst a group wait with suitcases to be collected at the end of their holiday (centre). In the background are the Sailor's Home Inn, Seaside Villas and Beach Villas of 1892.

▶ **LOWESTOFT**

Children's Corner c1945
L105070

Punch and Judy (centre right) first arrived in Lowestoft in 1886, but they moved to the south side of the pier in 1902. The Royal Hotel of 1849 is on the right, and in the distance are the villas along the Esplanade. These were all part of the mid-Victorian development of Lowestoft as a seaside resort by Sir Samuel Morton Peto of Somerleyton Hall.

◄ LOWESTOFT
*Punch and Judy,
Children's Corner
c1945* L105079

Franklin Spencer was
the Punch and Judy
man. His Punch voice
(produced by a device
held in his mouth
called a swazzle) was
amplified by means of
the loudspeaker to the
right of the stage.
The 1891 Pier Pavilion
(centre) stands at the
entrance to the pier,
and at the end of the
pier twin lighthouses
flank the harbour
mouth.

► LOWESTOFT
*The 'Centurion'
c1955* L105095

This is a wartime
motor fishing vessel
fitted up to look like
an 18th-century sailing
ship. The ship, which
visited many parts
around England, is
dressed with flags of
all nations, showing
the spread of the
Gospel throughout the
world. A mobile film
unit (its van stands to
the left of the ship) is
preparing to record
the event.

LOWESTOFT
The Pier, the Miniature Railway c1955 L105076

One of the most popular attractions on the seafront was the miniature railway, pulled by a Midlands Class 5 engine called 'Sonia'. In the background are the Harbour Hotel in London Road and the 1903 Royal Norfolk and Suffolk Yacht Club, paid for and opened by Lord Claud Hamilton, Chairman of the Great Eastern Railway Company.

▶ **LOWESTOFT**
The Harbour
c1955 L105072

The once flourishing herring fishery was already in decline at the time of this photograph. The trawlers have landed their catch, which is being cleaned, salted, packed and loaded into railway wagons. The large shop on the left is Tuttle's, the house furnisher's. The late Victorian terrace includes the Royal National Mission to Deep Sea Fishermen. On the right is the shingle mill, a vast screening plant, which was used to process shingle until 1958.

◀ **CORTON**
The Beach,
Rogerson Hall
Holiday Camp
c1960 C513041

Several holiday camps were built near Lowestoft in the post-war period. Rogerson Hall was always regarded as being more 'up-market' than the rest. The radar mast (left) was one of the chain-home low stations established by Watson Watt in 1938-39 to detect low-flying aircraft.

▲ **SOMERLEYTON,** *The Green c1955* S146010

Sir Samuel Morton Peto, the developer of Lowestoft, built these model cottages for his estate workers. Designed by John Thomas and erected between 1844 and 1851, the complex of 28 ornamental thatched or tiled picturesque cottages were situated overlooking a spacious green.

◄ **BECCLES**
High Street c1955
B45072

On the left is the jettied Falcon Inn, now a butcher's shop; Geoffrey Nudd next door, a tobacconist's, and Woolworth's have been rebuilt. The three gables over Hepworths have been removed. Ahead are Rayston's, selling high-class provisions, and Thompson's New Market Restaurant.

BECCLES
Exchange Square
c1955 B45055

On the left is the corner of Lloyds Bank; then comes Siddal and Kirby's shoe shop, the Wool Shop, now Nationwide with a new shop front, and the Midland Bank. To the right, the two boys are beside Ye Olde Shop; beyond it is the King's Head Hotel. Dewhurst the butchers are on the corner of Sheepsgate.

BECCLES, *New Market c1955* B45054

Morling's The House of Music (left) remains virtually unchanged. Masters & Stevens, the ironmonger's, has been rebuilt, and The Buttery (the white building) has been refitted. The Midland Bank on the right is now the Halifax. Vicomte François Chateaubriand, the French writer and diplomat, lived in exile next door from 1793 to 1795.

BECCLES
The River c1960
B45066

We are looking upstream, towards St Michael's Church, from the old quay; until the 1950s, Thames barges delivered grain here to Green's Mill. The iron bridge of c1880 replaced a medieval stone bridge. The Waveney forms the boundary between Suffolk and Norfolk, where the boys are fishing.

BUNGAY, *St Mary's Street c1960* B617023

The edge of St Mary's churchyard, with the war memorial in the form of a white cross, is on the right. The jettied building of c1500, on the left, was the Guildhall of the Mercers and Drapers. At this date it contains Sturgeon's, boot and shoe shop, and the International Stores.

► **BUNGAY**
Market Place
c1951 B617026

The two lorries, one of which is a Vulcan, are delivering to Reynold's grocery shop. Sharing the same building is Ellen Coustan, the ladies' and children's outfitter's. Both shops are now building societies. The board against the column of the 1689 Butter Cross (right) is advertising a Lambert's Coaches circular tour of Southwold and Lowestoft.

◄ **BUNGAY**
The Fleece Hotel c1955
B617013

The hotel, run by H Leighton, was described in1955 as being 'fully licensed, Adnams (Southwold) beers, large garage for cars'. Adjoining is the Georgian façade of the Pharmacy, which has lost its parapet and urns. Ahead is the Swan Inn, then run by A E Todd, now Sampson's Diner. To the right is H W Short's printing and stationery establishment.

▲ **BUNGAY,** *Earsham Street c1960* B617038

Whyte's high-class confectioners (left) is now Crocks. To the right is the red brick gabled London and Provincial Bank, and nearer to us is Mrs Carter's ladies' hairdresser's. Beyond the car was R Charlish, motor engineer and cycle agent. On either side of the road are the bus stops for the London to Lowestoft route.

◄ **BUNGAY**
Broad Street c1960
B617032

The policeman is approaching the portico of the former Mayfair Cinema, latterly called the Broadway until its closure. The mock-Tudor building opposite is Hunter & Olivers's the wine merchant's, based in Bury St Edmunds, now owned by Threshers.

MID SUFFOLK

METFIELD, *The Post Office c1965* M269010

The telephone box has gone, and the Post Office and shop, owned by R Boardman at this time, has closed, but the post box has become the letter box to the house. The shop was an extension to the 18th-century brick-fronted building. The house to the right has a panel with the Prince of Wales feathers.

LAXFIELD
Bridge Street c1955
L361005

On the corner of Low Road, leading to the King's Head, are houses called St Margaret and St Mary (centre left). The prominent jettied timber-framed building facing us is Waterloo House of c1540. To the right is the edge of the Endowed Infants School, rebuilt in 1859. Adjacent are Read's shop and the thatched Old Cycle Shop.

EYE, *Church Street c1960* E245005

On the left corner is Nunn's, the gents' outfitter's, which was hit by an unexploded bomb on 11 September 1940. The chemist's shop of J T Terry, with an exposed timber-framed wing, is now E Maynard's. Down the street the King's Head has closed, but retains its Lacon's sign on the wall. Set back is the Vine Church, a Baptist Chapel rebuilt in 1868.

EYE, *Broad Street c1960*
E245002

This area was once part of the market place, which was established between 1066 and 1072 outside the outer bailey of the castle. The buildings on the left were once market stalls, which developed into permanent shops. The monument is to Sir Edward Kerrison MP (1821-26) who 'promoted more institutions, organisations and public works than any other man in Suffolk'. The White Lion (right) closed in 1986.

▶ **DEBENHAM**
Cross Green c1955
D121004

The pump (left) stands on the corner of Low Street; the brick building opposite has been demolished. Ahead, below the church, is Bloomfield's engineering works – Bloomfield's were agents for Massey Harris machinery. To the left was Victor Last's blacksmith's shop. The church tower has Saxon quoins and Norman windows, with a rare west porch and Lady Chapel.

◀ **DEBENHAM**
High Street c1955
D121008

On the left is a Wealden-type house of c1400; it was restored in 1974-76. The Ancient Order of Foresters building of 1905 next door, which has Ionic columns, was designed by Raymond Wrinch of Ipswich. Opposite the Woolpack is Page's general stores, which became Websters in November 1958. At the top of the rise is Len Aldous, the saddler. The Victorian pump in the foreground is still there.

▲ **DEBENHAM,** *Market Green and High Street c1955* D121012

On the left is the jettied former Guildhall. At this end was Mark Ellis the tailor, later Fleming's Antiques; at the other end Barclays Bank. The sign is on the Red Lion (centre left), which closed in 2000. Opposite is H E Rose, the butcher. The market pump (right) stands outside Wright's newsagents shop. Nearer the painter on his ladder (extreme right) are a hardware shop and 'Granny' Clarke's general store.

◄ **DEBENHAM**
Market Square c1955
D121023

The wide shop on the left belongs to Henry Abbot, the long-established draper's, which became a Co-op in the late 1990s. Each alternate window on the first floor, has been blocked. The Victorian brick building (centre) was Carter's cycles and Wells's electrical shop. Next is Bond's fish and chips, with a sweet shop at the end of the row.

▼ **CLAYDON,** *Paper Mill Lane c1950* C510004

The thatched house with a brick front is The Rooks of c1620. The horse and trap are coming up Old Paper Mill Lane, which seems too narrow to have enabled the van and the trap to pass. All the buildings in the lane have been demolished; the site has been redeveloped and called Lime Kiln Close.

▶ **STOWMARKET**
Ipswich Street c1965
S583032

The first building on the left has been replaced by Boots. Juby's is now partly the post office. Gordon Ince's gents' outfitter's next door remains, whilst the Fox (beyond) has closed - its yard has been turned into a precinct. On the right is the forecourt of the Congregational Church, which was rebuilt in 1955 following its destruction by a German bomb in 1940.

◀ **STOWMARKET**
The Market c1965
S583039

This is Thursday, market day in Stowmarket. Stearn Brothers (straight ahead) had been a chemist's since the 1820s. It was owned by Stearn's from 1914 to 1922, but the name was retained until its closure in 1992. In the background is the Co-op furnishing department, trading as Vono.

▶ **OLD NEWTON**
Finningham Road
c1965 O97006

The Post Office has moved into three different buildings between here and the Shoulder of Mutton. The first, opposite the telephone box (in the distance on the right), was kept by Ella Kemp, the second was in the house with the posting box (centre). Its last location was in the new 1960s purpose-built Spar shop (left). The latter two were run by the Disney family. A garage has been added to this side of the shop.

GIPPING, *The Chapel c1955* G348011

The chapel of St Nicholas was built in the 1480s adjacent to his manor house by Sir James Tyrell. The nave and chancel are covered with external flushwork decorations, monograms, the Tyrell knot, and inscriptions, including one asking prayers for Sir James and Dame Ann. The tower, now rendered, was added in the Victorian period, and rather spoils the view.

ELMSWELL
The Post Office c1965
E171007

The house to the right was built c1965 by W A Leeks, who owned the adjacent Post Office and stores. Both were purchased by Tony Green in 1971, who in 1975 sold the store to Stowmarket Co-op. They have recently built a new store, which now virtually hides the Post Office.

BEYTON, *The White Horse Inn c1960* B877005

The drainpipe (right) marks the division between the timber-framed building of 1694 to the left and a Victorian brick extension nearer to us. Beyond the corner is a shop advertisement for Lyons Cakes. To the left was Rouse's cycle shop, a section of which was demolished to widen the road.

▶ **BEYTON**
The Village c1960 B877002

The school was built on the Green in 1872 at a cost of £700, with accommodation for 70 children. The side windows have gone and have been replaced by six sky-lights in the roof. The village pump is hidden in the long grass in front of the school. Little Paddock of c1600 stands at right angles to the track.

◄ **WALSHAM LE WILLOWS**
Summer Road c1960
W324018

This is one of several mock-Tudor cottages built by John Martineau for his workers. This pair are dated 1890, and the gable ends have inscriptions which read: 'Turn fortune turn thy wheel; with smile or frown; our hoard is little; but our hearts are great: Except the Lord build the House: their labour is but lost that built it'.

► **BOTESDALE**
The Village c1960 B619004

On the right is St Catherine's, reputedly the oldest house in the village, then Last's butcher's shop, once noted for its fine sausages, but now demolished. The gable on the left is Southgate Farm, the home of Eric and Emma Burroughes, the village wheelwright, whose work was featured in the film 'Requiem for the Village'.

◀ **RICKINGHALL**
The Street c1955 R327002

The fence marks the edge of Rickinghall Inferior churchyard, where a bus shelter was built c1960. Opposite, Bell Cottage and Wall Cottage are virtually unchanged. The cyclist is passing Mrs Davy's grocery and draper's shop at the corner of Parsonage Hill. Beyond the railway-like gate is the blacksmith's house.

FOREST
HEATH

BRANDON, *High Street c1955* B185001

The building with Gothic windows (far left) has been demolished. The shop next door still has a Cadburys chocolate advertisement on the window. Beyond the cars is the Baptist chapel of 1854. Opposite is Cabon & Son, a hairdresser's. The post office (right) is unchanged, but the telephone box has been replaced.

▶ **BRANDON**
The Flint Knappers,
Market Hill Corner
c1955 B185016

Brandon was famous for its flint knapping industry, which supplied gunflints throughout the world. The Edwardian pub retains many original features, including stained and lettered glass windows. P W Hyam's, opposite, baker and confectioner, has been demolished, along with all the buildings behind it. This was done when Brandon was redeveloped in the 1960 and 1970s, as a result of becoming a 'London Overspill' town.

◀ **LAKENHEATH**
High Street c1965
L362009

The 1922 war memorial (left) stands on a small green, where there were also trees and a pond until c1950. The shop front beyond belongs to Callis & Sons, a butcher's. On the right is the corner of the British Legion Hall, now much larger. At right angles is the Peace Memorial Hall of 1922, now a church, and beyond the National, now Central Garage.

▲ **ERISWELL,** *The Village c1960* E243005

Many of the houses here have the initials NEC, standing for the New England Company that once owned the parish. On the left is the post office, which closed in the 1980s, and the Chequers Inn. Opposite is Victoria Place, dated 1837, the year Queen Victoria came to the throne. The single-storey cottage has been converted to changing rooms for the sports field. At the corner of the metal fence is the village sign, unveiled by Bill Heffer.

◀**MILDENHALL**
Market Place
c1965 M75060

Friday has been the market day here since 1412. The base of the market cross is hidden by the stalls and the Victorian water pump. Ahead is the Tiger's Head and the Edwardian shoe shop of 1912. The magnificent 15th-century church tower dominates the Mildenhall skyline.

MILDENHALL
Market Place c1965
M75087

The market cross, similar to the one at Bungay, housed the stocks until the 19th century. The local Petty Sessions, empowered to place people in the stocks, sat in the nearby Bell Inn, which can be seen in photograph No M75059, below. Remington's stationer's and newsagent's is now part of a national chain.

MILDENHALL, *High Street c1965* M75059

The two shops on the left were both Morley's, one a clockmaker's, the other an ironmonger's. The tree is at the east end of the churchyard. The Bell (with a flagpole on the right) has been an inn since the 1790s. Barclays Bank is now to the right of the Bell. The taller building, beyond was Bussan & Parkin, an ironmonger's, until 1968.

BARTON MILLS
The Bull Inn c1965
B30002

There has been an inn here since at least 1680; it became a coaching inn in about 1750. This is the original front, which was built in two stages, the right half in 1680 and the left, with a carriage entrance, in about 1700. The entrance is now glazed to form a lounge. A white brick extension was built onto the left half in the 1920s.

EXNING, *Oxford Street c1955* E246001

The White Swan is on the right-hand corner. The postmaster stands in the doorway opposite; above is a sign for his billiard saloon. Posters advertise films at the Doric in Newmarket. Adjoining the post office is Enjoyable Cottage; then comes the roof of the Primary School, and Russell Villas of 1885. The furthest buildings were demolished in the 1970s.

NEWMARKET
High Street c1955
N23024

The lorry is parked outside the former Cockpit, dating from the 1660s. It later became part of the Fisher Theatre circuit from Norwich. Hammond's garage next door was called Rutland, after the nearby hotel. The pavement has since been extended to almost cover the whole area between here and Rouse Road.

▼ **NEWMARKET**, *The Roundabout c1955* N23029

The red brick clock tower of 1890 commemorates Queen Victoria's Golden Jubilee. On the left is Moon's cycle depot, connected with the garage in Bury Road. Mace's wireless shop is in Aberdeen House to the left, but their TV department is on the right-hand corner. In the background is the Rutland Arms Hotel.

▶ **NEWMARKET**

High Street c1955 N23001

The Rutland Arms Hotel, designed by John Kent, was built in 1815 on the site of the Ram Inn. The side against the High Street has the Duke's coat of arms in the pediment. Opposite is the 16th-century Wagon and Horses, in whose yard the livestock market used to be held.

NEWMARKET
High Street c1955
N23003

The Carlton Hotel with its cupola (right) dominated the High Street. It was demolished in 1977 and replaced by Boots. To the left is Musks, butcher and sausage makers, displaying their Royal Warrants. The rest of the group, including the Congregational Church of 1863, were demolished in the 1960s, when a new church was built on the site.

NEWMARKET
High Street c1955
N23011

On the left is the Electricity Centre; Selright, a ladies' fashion shop; Topping's shoe shop; and Anscombes the photographer's. The delicate cresting over the shops has gone. The lower building marks Grosvenor Yard. Beyond are the semi-circular front of the 1930s Doric Cinema and the gable of King Edward VII Memorial Hall.

NEWMARKET
Race-horses Crossing the Main Road c1955 N23036

Until the A14 (then the A45) by-pass was opened, this was a familiar scene for motorists leaving Suffolk. This crossing is at the east end of Bury Road, with No 58 visible through the trees, just west of the traffic lights and junction of the roads from Bury and Norwich. These crossings added much time to early and mid-morning journeys.

95

ST EDMUNDSBURY

▲ **IXWORTH,** *High Street c1965* I76054

The shop with the delicate early 19th-century windows (left) is J F Ferguson's London House Stores, now a restaurant. Opposite is Ixworth Dairy, with a Gothic shop front. The large house is The Beeches, and beyond it is the office of Mulley's Motorways. This firm ran local bus and coach services from 1939 until 1975. The vintage coaches were often used in the 'Dad's Army' TV series.

▶ **CONYERS GREEN**
The Farm c1960
C747008

This former farmhouse, which dates from the 1480s, has a double jetty in the right cross wing. The central section still has remains of the open hall. The front has Edwardian mock timbering. The barn to the left is now a house called The Flints, in front of which part of the pond has been filled in.

◀ BURY ST EDMUNDS
Angel Hill c1955
B258008

The Athenaeum (centre), which was re-fronted in 1802-04, has a Victorian observatory on the roof. The Art Deco illuminated direction sign (left), known locally as the 'Pillar of Salt', dates from 1935. The famous Angel Hotel, mentioned in Dickens' 'Pickwick Papers', is to the right. To the left are Abbey House, the Cathedral, the Norman tower and St Mary's.

▶ BURY ST EDMUNDS
The Butter Market c1965 B258095

The Suffolk Hotel (right) has closed; the façade has been retained, and the building has been converted into two shops. The building with a gable beyond replaced an earlier one destroyed in a Zeppelin raid in 1915. Ahead is Moyses Hall, one of the oldest domestic buildings in England, built c1180. Market days in Bury are Wednesday and Saturday.

BURY ST EDMUNDS
*Abbey Gate and
Angel Hill c1960* B258072

The abbey gate replaced a
Norman gate destroyed by
the townspeople in 1327,
who then had to pay for
this castle-like defensive
structure. Buses parked near
the war memorial and the
Pillar of Salt (left) belong to
the private companies
providing rural services.

BURY ST EDMUNDS
Cornhill c1965 B258001

The Greene King dray (left) is outside Everard's Hotel, which closed in 1987. On the right is the Corn Exchange of 1861, now with shops on the ground floor. Beyond is the Provisions Market of 1834, later the School of Art, fire station and library, now also shops. On the left, half way along, are the Art Deco Burtons of 1933 and Boot's mock-Tudor shop of 1913.

HAVERHILL
High Street c1965
H381016

We are looking north towards the church. On the right, we can see the carriage entrance of the Red Lion next to Carter's the jeweller's; further on is Barclays Bank, which was re-fronted in 1822. The high gable on the left is Helions House surgery, now Woolworth's. The pushchair is outside Huggins's shop.

HAVERHILL, *High Street c1965* H381047

This was taken from the corner of the churchyard. The former Corn Exchange of 1857 is on the left, obscuring the Market Hill Chapel of 1839. Stanwoods (centre right) is the former Chantry House of the Gurteen family, great employers and benefactors in the town. The 1950s Boots (left) is on the site of the Anchor Temperance Coffee Tavern. The taller building is Atterton & Ellis, an ironmonger's.

HAVERHILL, *Queen's Square c1965* H381052

In the early 1960s Haverhill was named the Pioneer of Town Expansion, thanks to its receiving 'London Overspill' industries and workers. The provision of new facilities and shops was a priority, and in consequence many areas were demolished. These harsh new concrete structures replaced shops on this side of Queen Street - the retention of an old lamp-post (with a new top) does little to compensate.

103

▶ **CLARE**
Callis Street c1960
C512004

The Cock Inn and Peterhouse (left) are 17th-century buildings. The Cock, run by H Painter, has a later door case, and Peterhouse has a Victorian shop window. The Globe Inn, beyond, run by Mrs Stiff, is 18th-century, but re-fronted in the 19th century. The County Primary School is set back behind the Globe.

◀ **CAVENDISH**
The Green c1965 C509012

The brick house on the left belonged to the blacksmith, with the forge behind.
A house has since been built in the yard. To the right is the Grape Vine of c1520, with 20th-century pargetting. The White Horse, beyond, is 18th-century with a mansard roof. Opposite is Green End, re-fronted in white brick in the 1860s, with the names of the workmen cut into the bricks by the front door.

BABERGH

HARTEST, *The Green c1960* H380010

To the right of the picture are the Hall, now the Crown Inn, and the church. Behind the war memorial is Church House, the former Guildhall. Hartest Hill rises steeply with the Plymouth Brethren Gospel Hall, which closed in 1977, on the right and the cemetery of 1857 on the left. On the edge of the green are the former wheelwright's house and workshop.

GLEMSFORD
Tye Green c1960
G235005

In the centre is the general store with a fish and chip shop, then owned by D A Chatters. The water tower behind the thatched cottage has since been demolished. One of the two houses on the left belonged to Seabrook's Farm, and the other was the vicarage. This was occupied by the Rev Harpur, who was here from 1937 to 1950, and after whom the nearby road was named.

SUDBURY, *Market Hill and St Peter's Church c1965* S472035

St Peter's Church is now redundant. The statue of Thomas Gainsborough, the artist, was erected in front of the tower in 1913. On the left is the Bank of 1903, with columns between the windows and circular fanlights. Amongst all the national chain stores on the left are E W King's high-class grocer's and F W Page's ironmonger's. The market is held here on Saturdays.

◄ LAVENHAM
Water Street c1955
L21012

The stream which rises at Lavenham Hall used to flow here, but now it runs in a brick culvert underground. De Vere House, on the right, which was largely dismantled and rebuilt in the 1920s, has gables, jetties, oriel windows and brick nogging. The de Vere star and boar are carved in the spandrels of the doorway. Beyond are three rows of once jettied cottages.

SUDBURY
*Friars Street
c1960* S472047

The Dominican friars established a Friary here before 1247, hence the street name. On the right the low wall is in front of the Congregational church, now demolished. Several of the houses have later façades. The central one is where Thomas Gainsborough lived in the 1750s.

▲ **LAVENHAM,** *Lady Street c1960* L21008

On the left is a high-quality Tudor house, with arched windows for a shop at the far end. Opposite is the 15th-century Wool Hall, originally the Guild of Our Lady, with an open hall and cross-wings. It was dismantled in 1911, but local opposition prevented its removal and it is now part of the Swan. At the end is Priory Farm, which once belonged to Earls Colne in Essex.

BRENT ELEIGH
The Village c1960
B615006

Both the Post Office, now Swan Cottage and Tudor Cottage date from the 17th century. The larger house with the dramatic jetty (centre) is Highbank, a medieval hall house. The thatched extension at this end has been demolished. The imposing brick building beyond is the Colman Almshouses of 1731. The River Brett flows parallel to the street on the right.

▶ **BILDESTON**
The Clock Tower c1960 B766012

This was built in 1864. Its only clock dial faces Albert Hall's grocer's and draper's shop (left), now Bank House Stores. The house on the corner of Chapel Street (centre) now has a porch in the second bay. Still's stores (right) later became Simpson's antique shop, and since 1990 it has been a private house.

▼ **KERSEY**
The Ford and the Church c1955
K136008

The name Kersey means 'cress island', a fact to contemplate when crossing the Brett by bridge or ford. At the top of the hill is one of the best-known views in Suffolk. On the left, Bridge House has a shop window from a former sweet shop. Across the bridge, Ye Olde River House is dated 1490.

▶ **HADLEIGH**
High Street c1955
H2011

The 18th-century obelisk milestone (centre left) was moved to outside the George in 1974. The building on the right has 17th-century pargetting, with the arms of Bayning. Hicks, on the left, has an original 15th-century door. Beyond the George (centre right) is the premises of M W Partridge, the ironmonger for this area of Suffolk.

◀ **HADLEIGH**
High Street c1965
H2028

Queen Street on the right, built in 1838, leads to the churchyard. The tall building (centre) with carved bargeboards, dormer windows, ridge tiles and 'Tudor' chimneys was Boots.
The Betabake van (left) stands outside the Coffee Tavern of 1676, which has six Venetian windows on the first floor. Near to us, with the awning, is the Co-op.

EAST BERGHOLT
The Village c1955
E247030

The 17th-century Red Lion (right) was a Cobbold pub, run by J E Smith. The single-storey extension hides the Old Manse, the post office and John Constable's first studio. At the end of the street, the petrol pumps have gone, and Thrower's the newsagent's has become an estate agent's. Opposite is Hatters, where straw hats were made.

SHOTLEY GATE, *The Jetties c1955* S581004

To the right is a destroyer of the Reserve Fleet; in the centre is the Naval Dry Dock; and to the left is the Harwich to Hook of Holland ferry. The landing stage and boats were part of the Naval Training Establishment HMS Ganges. Originally this was a training ship, but it became land based from 1905 until 1976. During this time over 150,000 naval ratings were trained at Shotley.

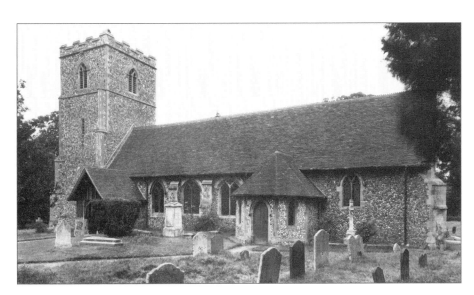

FRESTON
The Church c1955
F144001

Freston is well known for the Freston Elizabethan tower overlooking the estuary, the Boot public house, and the parish church. This was restored in 1875 and faced with beach pebbles, and a curious vestry was added to the south side. Internally the beams that supported the rood screen can still be seen.

IPSWICH, *Tavern Street c1955* I18036

On the corner is the Great White Horse Hotel (right), where Dickens' Mr Pickwick, returning to the wrong room, disturbed a lady wearing yellow curling papers. Opposite, the Victorian buildings contain Kendall's, the Co-op Insurance and, with the clock, Croyden's the jeweller's. In the distance is the Town Hall clock tower.

IPSWICH
The Town Hall c1955
I18053

The Town Hall, with the clock tower, was built on the Cornhill in 1867. It was designed in the Italian style by Bellamy and Hardy of Lincoln, with figures of Justice, Learning, Agriculture and Commerce standing below the Borough Arms. The adjacent post office was erected in 1881, with statues of Industry, Electricity, Steam and Commerce standing below the Royal Arms.

IPSWICH, *The Ancient House c1955* I18017

The cinema (left) offers 'Easter Parade' with Judy Garland and Fred Astaire, or a boxing match between Freddy Mills and Joe Woodcock. The Ancient House next door is 16th-century, but was re-fronted in c1670. The arms of Charles II are in the centre of four elaborate oriel windows, with pargetting representing four continents.

INDEX

Frith Book Co Titles

www.francisfrith.co.uk

The Frith Book Company publishes over 100 new titles each year. A selection of those currently available is listed below. For latest catalogue please contact Frith Book Co.
Town Books 96 pages, approximately 100 photos. **County and Themed Books** 128 pages, approximately 150 photos (unless specified). All titles hardback with laminated case and jacket, except those indicated pb (paperback)

Amersham, Chesham & Rickmansworth (pb)	1-85937-340-2	£9.99	Devon (pb)	1-85937-297-x	£9.99
Andover (pb)	1-85937-292-9	£9.99	Devon Churches (pb)	1-85937-250-3	£9.99
Aylesbury (pb)	1-85937-227-9	£9.99	Dorchester (pb)	1-85937-307-0	£9.99
Barnstaple (pb)	1-85937-300-3	£9.99	Dorset (pb)	1-85937-269-4	£9.99
Basildon Living Memories (pb)	1-85937-515-4	£9.99	Dorset Coast (pb)	1-85937-299-6	£9.99
Bath (pb)	1-85937-419-0	£9.99	Dorset Living Memories (pb)	1-85937-584-7	£9.99
Bedford (pb)	1-85937-205-8	£9.99	Down the Severn (pb)	1-85937-560-x	£9.99
Bedfordshire Living Memories	1-85937-513-8	£14.99	Down The Thames (pb)	1-85937-278-3	£9.99
Belfast (pb)	1-85937-303-8	£9.99	Down the Trent	1-85937-311-9	£14.99
Berkshire (pb)	1-85937-191-4	£9.99	East Anglia (pb)	1-85937-265-1	£9.99
Berkshire Churches	1-85937-170-1	£17.99	East Grinstead (pb)	1-85937-138-8	£9.99
Berkshire Living Memories	1-85937-332-1	£14.99	East London	1-85937-080-2	£14.99
Black Country	1-85937-497-2	£12.99	East Sussex (pb)	1-85937-606-1	£9.99
Blackpool (pb)	1-85937-393-3	£9.99	Eastbourne (pb)	1-85937-399-2	£9.99
Bognor Regis (pb)	1-85937-431-x	£9.99	Edinburgh (pb)	1-85937-193-0	£8.99
Bournemouth (pb)	1-85937-545-6	£9.99	England In The 1880s	1-85937-331-3	£17.99
Bradford (pb)	1-85937-204-x	£9.99	Essex - Second Selection	1-85937-456-5	£14.99
Bridgend (pb)	1-85937-386-0	£7.99	Essex (pb)	1-85937-270-8	£9.99
Bridgwater (pb)	1-85937-305-4	£9.99	Essex Coast	1-85937-342-9	£14.99
Bridport (pb)	1-85937-327-5	£9.99	Essex Living Memories	1-85937-490-5	£14.99
Brighton (pb)	1-85937-192-2	£8.99	Exeter	1-85937-539-1	£9.99
Bristol (pb)	1-85937-264-3	£9.99	Exmoor (pb)	1-85937-608-8	£9.99
British Life A Century Ago (pb)	1-85937-213-9	£9.99	Falmouth (pb)	1-85937-594-4	£9.99
Buckinghamshire (pb)	1-85937-200-7	£9.99	Folkestone (pb)	1-85937-124-8	£9.99
Camberley (pb)	1-85937-222-8	£9.99	Frome (pb)	1-85937-317-8	£9.99
Cambridge (pb)	1-85937-422-0	£9.99	Glamorgan	1-85937-488-3	£14.99
Cambridgeshire (pb)	1-85937-420-4	£9.99	Glasgow (pb)	1-85937-190-6	£9.99
Cambridgeshire Villages	1-85937-523-5	£14.99	Glastonbury (pb)	1-85937-338-0	£7.99
Canals And Waterways (pb)	1-85937-291-0	£9.99	Gloucester (pb)	1-85937-232-5	£9.99
Canterbury Cathedral (pb)	1-85937-179-5	£9.99	Gloucestershire (pb)	1-85937-561-8	£9.99
Cardiff (pb)	1-85937-093-4	£9.99	Great Yarmouth (pb)	1-85937-426-3	£9.99
Carmarthenshire (pb)	1-85937-604-7	£9.99	Greater Manchester (pb)	1-85937-266-x	£9.99
Chelmsford (pb)	1-85937-310-0	£9.99	Guildford (pb)	1-85937-410-7	£9.99
Cheltenham (pb)	1-85937-095-0	£9.99	Hampshire (pb)	1-85937-279-1	£9.99
Cheshire (pb)	1-85937-271-6	£9.99	Harrogate (pb)	1-85937-423-9	£9.99
Chester (pb)	1-85937-382 8	£9.99	Hastings and Bexhill (pb)	1-85937-131-0	£9.99
Chesterfield (pb)	1-85937-378-x	£9.99	Heart of Lancashire (pb)	1-85937-197-3	£9.99
Chichester (pb)	1-85937-228-7	£9.99	Helston (pb)	1-85937-214-7	£9.99
Churches of East Cornwall (pb)	1-85937-249-x	£9.99	Hereford (pb)	1-85937-175-2	£9.99
Churches of Hampshire (pb)	1-85937-207-4	£9.99	Herefordshire (pb)	1-85937-567-7	£9.99
Cinque Ports & Two Ancient Towns	1-85937-492-1	£14.99	Herefordshire Living Memories	1-85937-514-6	£14.99
Colchester (pb)	1-85937-188-4	£8.99	Hertfordshire (pb)	1-85937-247-3	£9.99
Cornwall (pb)	1-85937-229-5	£9.99	Horsham (pb)	1-85937-432-8	£9.99
Cornwall Living Memories	1-85937-248-1	£14.99	Humberside (pb)	1-85937-605-3	£9.99
Cotswolds (pb)	1-85937-230-9	£9.99	Hythe, Romney Marsh, Ashford (pb)	1-85937-256-2	£9.99
Cotswolds Living Memories	1-85937-255-4	£14.99	Ipswich (pb)	1-85937-424-7	£9.99
County Durham (pb)	1-85937-398-4	£9.99	Isle of Man (pb)	1-85937-268-6	£9.99
Croydon Living Memories (pb)	1-85937-162-0	£9.99	Isle of Wight (pb)	1-85937-429-8	£9.99
Cumbria (pb)	1-85937-621-5	£9.99	Isle of Wight Living Memories	1-85937-304-6	£14.99
Derby (pb)	1-85937-367-4	£9.99	Kent (pb)	1-85937-189-2	£9.99
Derbyshire (pb)	1-85937-196-5	£9.99	Kent Living Memories(pb)	1-85937-401-8	£9.99
Derbyshire Living Memories	1-85937-330-5	£14.99	Kings Lynn (pb)	1-85937-334-8	£9.99

Available from your local bookshop or from the publisher

Frith Book Co Titles (continued)

Lake District (pb)	1-85937-275-9	£9.99	Sherborne (pb)	1-85937-301-1	£9.99
Lancashire Living Memories	1-85937-335-6	£14.99	Shrewsbury (pb)	1-85937-325-9	£9.99
Lancaster, Morecambe, Heysham (pb)	1-85937-233-3	£9.99	Shropshire (pb)	1-85937-326-7	£9.99
Leeds (pb)	1-85937-202-3	£9.99	Shropshire Living Memories	1-85937-643-6	£14.99
Leicester (pb)	1-85937-381-x	£9.99	Somerset	1-85937-153-1	£14.99
Leicestershire & Rutland Living Memories	1-85937-500-6	£12.99	South Devon Coast	1-85937-107-8	£14.99
Leicestershire (pb)	1-85937-185-x	£9.99	South Devon Living Memories (pb)	1-85937-609-6	£9.99
Lighthouses	1-85937-257-0	£9.99	South East London (pb)	1-85937-263-5	£9.99
Lincoln (pb)	1-85937-380-1	£9.99	South Somerset	1-85937-318-6	£14.99
Lincolnshire (pb)	1-85937-433-6	£9.99	South Wales	1-85937-519-7	£14.99
Liverpool and Merseyside (pb)	1-85937-234-1	£9.99	Southampton (pb)	1-85937-427-1	£9.99
London (pb)	1-85937-183-3	£9.99	Southend (pb)	1-85937-313-5	£9.99
London Living Memories	1-85937-454-9	£14.99	Southport (pb)	1-85937-425-5	£9.99
Ludlow (pb)	1-85937-176-0	£9.99	St Albans (pb)	1-85937-341-0	£9.99
Luton (pb)	1-85937-235-x	£9.99	St Ives (pb)	1-85937-415-8	£9.99
Maidenhead (pb)	1-85937-339-9	£9.99	Stafford Living Memories (pb)	1-85937-503-0	£9.99
Maidstone (pb)	1-85937-391-7	£9.99	Staffordshire (pb)	1-85937-308-9	£9.99
Manchester (pb)	1-85937-198-1	£9.99	Stourbridge (pb)	1-85937-530-8	£9.99
Marlborough (pb)	1-85937-336-4	£9.99	Stratford upon Avon (pb)	1-85937-388-7	£9.99
Middlesex	1-85937-158-2	£14.99	Suffolk (pb)	1-85937-221-x	£9.99
Monmouthshire	1-85937-532-4	£14.99	Suffolk Coast (pb)	1-85937-610-x	£9.99
New Forest (pb)	1-85937-390-9	£9.99	Surrey (pb)	1-85937-240-6	£9.99
Newark (pb)	1-85937-366-6	£9.99	Surrey Living Memories	1-85937-328-3	£14.99
Newport, Wales (pb)	1-85937-258-9	£9.99	Sussex (pb)	1-85937-184-1	£9.99
Newquay (pb)	1-85937-421-2	£9.99	Sutton (pb)	1-85937-337-2	£9.99
Norfolk (pb)	1-85937-195-7	£9.99	Swansea (pb)	1-85937-167-1	£9.99
Norfolk Broads	1-85937-486-7	£14.99	Taunton (pb)	1-85937-314-3	£9.99
Norfolk Living Memories (pb)	1-85937-402-6	£9.99	Tees Valley & Cleveland (pb)	1-85937-623-1	£9.99
North Buckinghamshire	1-85937-626-6	£14.99	Teignmouth (pb)	1-85937-370-4	£7.99
North Devon Living Memories	1-85937-261-9	£14.99	Thanet (pb)	1-85937-116-7	£9.99
North Hertfordshire	1-85937-547-2	£14.99	Tiverton (pb)	1-85937-178-7	£9.99
North London (pb)	1-85937-403-4	£9.99	Torbay (pb)	1-85937-597-9	£9.99
North Somerset	1-85937-302-x	£14.99	Truro (pb)	1-85937-598-7	£9.99
North Wales (pb)	1-85937-298-8	£9.99	Victorian & Edwardian Dorset	1-85937-254-6	£14.99
North Yorkshire (pb)	1-85937-236-8	£9.99	Victorian & Edwardian Kent (pb)	1-85937-624-X	£9.99
Northamptonshire Living Memories	1-85937-529-4	£14.99	Victorian & Edwardian Maritime Album (pb)	1-85937-622-3	£9.99
Northamptonshire	1-85937-150-7	£14.99	Victorian and Edwardian Sussex (pb)	1-85937-625-8	£9.99
Northumberland Tyne & Wear (pb)	1-85937-281-3	£9.99	Villages of Devon (pb)	1-85937-293-7	£9.99
Northumberland	1-85937-522-7	£14.99	Villages of Kent (pb)	1-85937-294-5	£9.99
Norwich (pb)	1-85937-194-9	£8.99	Villages of Sussex (pb)	1-85937-295-3	£9.99
Nottingham (pb)	1-85937-324-0	£9.99	Warrington (pb)	1-85937-507-3	£9.99
Nottinghamshire (pb)	1-85937-187-6	£9.99	Warwick (pb)	1-85937-518-9	£9.99
Oxford (pb)	1-85937-411-5	£9.99	Warwickshire (pb)	1-85937-203-1	£9.99
Oxfordshire (pb)	1-85937-430-1	£9.99	Welsh Castles (pb)	1-85937-322-4	£9.99
Oxfordshire Living Memories	1-85937-525-1	£14.99	West Midlands (pb)	1-85937-289-9	£9.99
Paignton (pb)	1-85937-374-7	£7.99	West Sussex (pb)	1-85937-607-x	£9.99
Peak District (pb)	1-85937-280-5	£9.99	West Yorkshire (pb)	1-85937-201-5	£9.99
Pembrokeshire	1-85937-262-7	£14.99	Weston Super Mare (pb)	1-85937-306-2	£9.99
Penzance (pb)	1-85937-595-2	£9.99	Weymouth (pb)	1-85937-209-0	£9.99
Peterborough (pb)	1-85937-219-8	£9.99	Wiltshire (pb)	1-85937-277-5	£9.99
Picturesque Harbours	1-85937-208-2	£14.99	Wiltshire Churches (pb)	1-85937-171-x	£9.99
Piers	1-85937-237-6	£17.99	Wiltshire Living Memories (pb)	1-85937-396-8	£9.99
Plymouth (pb)	1-85937-389-5	£9.99	Winchester (pb)	1-85937-428-x	£9.99
Poole & Sandbanks (pb)	1-85937-251-1	£9.99	Windsor (pb)	1-85937-333-x	£9.99
Preston (pb)	1-85937-212-0	£9.99	Wokingham & Bracknell (pb)	1-85937-329-1	£9.99
Reading (pb)	1-85937-238-4	£9.99	Woodbridge (pb)	1-85937-498-0	£9.99
Redhill to Reigate (pb)	1-85937-596-0	£9.99	Worcester (pb)	1-85937-165-5	£9.99
Ringwood (pb)	1-85937-384-4	£7.99	Worcestershire Living Memories	1-85937-489-1	£14.99
Romford (pb)	1-85937-319-4	£9.99	Worcestershire	1-85937-152-3	£14.99
Royal Tunbridge Wells (pb)	1-85937-504-9	£9.99	York (pb)	1-85937-199-x	£9.99
Salisbury (pb)	1-85937-239-2	£9.99	Yorkshire (pb)	1-85937-186-8	£9.99
Scarborough (pb)	1-85937-379-8	£9.99	Yorkshire Coastal Memories	1-85937-506-5	£14.99
Sevenoaks and Tonbridge (pb)	1-85937-392-5	£9.99	Yorkshire Dales	1-85937-502-2	£14.99
Sheffield & South Yorks (pb)	1-85937-267-8	£9.99	Yorkshire Living Memories (pb)	1-85937-397-6	£9.99

See Frith books on the internet at www.francisfrith.co.uk

FRITH PRODUCTS & SERVICES

Francis Frith would doubtless be pleased to know that the pioneering publishing venture he started in 1860 still continues today. Over a hundred and forty years later, The Francis Frith Collection continues in the same innovative tradition and is now one of the foremost publishers of vintage photographs in the world. Some of the current activities include:

Interior Decoration

Today Frith's photographs can be seen framed and as giant wall murals in thousands of pubs, restaurants, hotels, banks, retail stores and other public buildings throughout the country. In every case they enhance the unique local atmosphere of the places they depict and provide reminders of gentler days in an increasingly busy and frenetic world.

Product Promotions

Frith products are used by many major companies to promote the sales of their own products or to reinforce their own history and heritage. Frith promotions have been used by Hovis bread, Courage beers, Scots Porage Oats, Colman's mustard, Cadbury's foods, Mellow Birds coffee, Dunhill pipe tobacco, Guinness, and Bulmer's Cider.

Genealogy and Family History

As the interest in family history and roots grows world-wide, more and more people are turning to Frith's photographs of Great Britain for images of the towns, villages and streets where their ancestors lived; and, of course, photographs of the churches and chapels where their ancestors were christened, married and buried are an essential part of every genealogy tree and family album.

Frith Products

All Frith photographs are available Framed or just as Mounted Prints and Posters (size 23 x 16 inches). These may be ordered from the address below. From time to time other products - Address Books, Calendars, Table Mats, etc - are available.

The Internet

Already fifty thousand Frith photographs can be viewed and purchased on the internet through the Frith websites and a myriad of partner sites.

For more detailed information on Frith companies and products, look at these sites:

www.francisfrith.co.uk
www.francisfrith.com
(for North American visitors)

See the complete list of Frith Books at:

www.francisfrith.co.uk

This web site is regularly updated with the latest list of publications from the Frith Book Company. If you wish to buy books relating to another part of the country that your local bookshop does not stock, you may purchase on-line.

For further information, trade, or author enquiries please contact us at the address below:
The Francis Frith Collection, Frith's Barn, Teffont, Salisbury, Wiltshire, England SP3 5QP.
Tel: +44 (0) 1722 716 376 Fax: +44 (0) 1722 716 881 Email: sales@francisfrith.co.uk

See Frith books on the internet at www.francisfrith.co.uk

FREE PRINT OF YOUR CHOICE

Mounted Print
Overall size 14 x 11 inches (355 x 280mm)

Choose any Frith photograph in this book.
Simply complete the Voucher opposite and return it with your remittance for £2.25 (to cover postage and handling) and we will print the photograph of your choice in SEPIA (size 11 x 8 inches) and supply it in a cream mount with a burgundy rule line (overall size 14 x 11 inches).
Please note: photographs with a reference number starting with a "Z" are not Frith photographs and cannot be supplied under this offer.
Offer valid for delivery to UK addresses only.

PLUS: Order additional Mounted Prints at HALF PRICE - £7.49 each (normally £14.99)
If you would like to order more Frith prints from this book, possibly as gifts for friends and family, you can buy them at half price (with no additional postage and handling costs).

PLUS: Have your Mounted Prints framed
For an extra £14.95 per print you can have your mounted print(s) framed in an elegant polished wood and gilt moulding, overall size 16 x 13 inches (no additional postage and handling required).

IMPORTANT!

These special prices are only available if you use this form to order `3`. You must use the ORIGINAL VOUCHER on this page (no copies permitted). We can only despatch to one address. This offer cannot be combined with any other offer.

Send completed Voucher form to:
The Francis Frith Collection, Frith's Barn, Teffont, Salisbury, Wiltshire SP3 5QP

CHOOSE A PHOTOGRAPH FROM THIS BOOK

Voucher for **FREE** and Reduced Price Frith Prints

Please do not photocopy this voucher. Only the original is valid, so please fill it in, cut it out and return it to us with your order.

Picture ref no	Page no	Qty	Mounted @ £7.49	Framed + £14.95	Total Cost
		1	Free of charge*	£	£
			£7.49	£	£
			£7.49	£	£
			£7.49	£	£
			£7.49	£	£
			£7.49	£	£
Please allow 28 days for delivery			* Post & handling (UK)	£2.25	
			Total Order Cost	£	

Title of this book . . . .
I enclose a cheque/postal order for £ . . . .
made payable to 'The Francis Frith Collection'

OR please debit my Mastercard / Visa / Switch (Maestro) /Amex card
(credit cards please on all overseas orders), details below

Card Number

Issue No (Switch only)   Valid from (Amex/Switch)

Expires   Signature

Name Mr/Mrs/Ms . . . .
Address . . . .
. . . .
. . . .
. . . . Postcode . . . .
Daytime Tel No . . . .
Email . . . .

Valid to 31/12/07

Would you like to find out more about Francis Frith?

We have recently recruited some entertaining speakers who are happy to visit local groups, clubs and societies to give an illustrated talk documenting Frith's travels and photographs. If you are a member of such a group and are interested in hosting a presentation, we would love to hear from you.

Our speakers bring with them a small selection of our local town and county books, together with sample prints. They are happy to take orders. A small proportion of the order value is donated to the group who have hosted the presentation. The talks are therefore an excellent way of fundraising for small groups and societies.

Can you help us with information about any of the Frith photographs in this book?

We are gradually compiling an historical record for each of the photographs in the Frith archive. It is always fascinating to find out the names of the people shown in the pictures, as well as insights into the shops, buildings and other features depicted.

If you recognize anyone in the photographs in this book, or if you have information not already included in the author's caption, do let us know. We would love to hear from you, and will try to publish it in future books or articles.

Our production team

Frith books are produced by a small dedicated team at offices in the converted Grade II listed 18th-century barn at Teffont near Salisbury, illustrated above. Most have worked with the Frith Collection for many years. All have in common one quality: they have a passion for the Frith Collection. The team is constantly expanding, but currently includes:

Paul Baron, Phillip Brennan, Jason Buck, John Buck, Ruth Butler, Heather Crisp, David Davies, Louis du Mont, Isobel Hall, Gareth Harris, Lucy Hart, Julian Hight, Peter Horne, James Kinnear, Karen Kinnear, Tina Leary, Stuart Login, David Marsh, Lesley-Ann Millard, Sue Molloy, Glenda Morgan, Wayne Morgan, Sarah Roberts, Kate Rotondetto, Dean Scource, Eliza Sackett, Terence Sackett, Sandra Sampson, Adrian Sanders, Sandra Sanger, Jan Scrivens, Julia Skinner, David Smith, Miles Smith, Lewis Taylor, Shelley Tolcher, Lorraine Tuck, Amanita Wainwright and Ricky Williams.